Heavy Sublimation: New Poems

Leonard Schwartz

HEAVY SUBLIMATION : NEW POEMS

Talisman House, Publishers • 2018
Northfield, Massachusetts

Published in the United States of America by
Talisman House, Publishers
P.O. Box 102
Northfield, Massachusetts 01360

11 12 13 7 6 5 4 3 2 1 First Edition

Manufactured in the United States of America
Printed on acid-free paper

ISBN: 978-1-58498-132-9

Some of these poems first appeared in *Or, The Brooklyn Rail, Hambone, Rascal,
The Spoon River Poetry Review, Talisman,* and *Verse.*

Front cover: Peter Hristoff, *Everything and Nothing: Expulsion* 2007 - 2016, mixed media
on paper. Courtesy of the artist and C.A.M. Gallery, Istanbul. Photo: Jean Vong

CONTENTS

CAPITOL FOREST

1

ONE, the top of which
Blown off

By its own
Volcanic force.

The other tumescent.
Intact. Seemingly overdue.

CLIFF turned to
Quarry, now abandoned

So many
Scattering rocks:

Make believe hermitage
In the fragile.

AMAZINGLY
A raven is

Heard in this
Turbulent border

Between
Telos and boredom.

SADLY, we are all wise.
Appearances really are

Mere appearances and
A thermos of water

Imagines itself
Superior to rain.

2

One has a rim
Blown asunder.

The other whirls
Intact.

Elation fails to anoint
A metaphor to overflow

The terms
Of its comparison...

One is panic
In the road...

Storm clouds
Refusing to be stanched...

The ripped *parapluie* of our hearts
The rain pelts...

And...
And...

A downpour applauds
The lovers

For their early
Morning contact.

Leaves as large
As a mead hall

Wetly envelop
The house.

3

Behind phonemes
Are pheromones and

Behind pheromones
Are forms

Fruit, letters
And trunks.

Now the density
Of air

In the lion's
Den, now a hand on a

Feverish
Forehead.

Now snow flakes
Fall on snowflakes.

Specks
We embrace/

Mists enfolding
Domestic hearth.

Now-again reading into the night
Across our several screens.

Lacking the ability to locate
One's own black box

One studies the logs
Of somebody else's last minutes.

Image flees from object
Like smoke from a stick.

In addition, is the incense of that thing?
In addition, its diffusion into other senses.

    4

At the border between
Telos and boredom

Rain pounds
The unmoving raven.

Crows come:
The raven flinches.

Logs crash together
In our welling eyes,

Tidal improvisations
Beyond our control

As anxiety is many rivulets
In addition, anguish is an assaulted river

In addition, large round lights tremble
Along a silken pathway.

To traverse a long distance correctly
And a short distance incorrectly

Such that a fen
Holds me tightly

In welling isolation
In addition, ominous mud.

Barely perceivable bodies
Move over the house.

5

One altered
The planet's weather.

The other
Will.

Bound together
Intention and driftwood

The size of
Naked tree trunks

Thunder in
Our eyes.

Imitate me
Says the opossum

On his death bed
Of pine needles and wine.

Fibers in the toothpick
Squirm away from my gum

Yearning for the tree
They came from

Maybe the tree
By the pond

By which we once
Made out

With much oral
Celebration.

Freedom, as frail
As skin, as abused

As a nervous system
In submission to Big Pharma

Flashes for a moment
When new conversation buds.

The mind will not be condensed
Into a few small drops.

Nature, ultimately, means everything,
Not just one newt with poisonous skin

But night and day
And everything in them.

In other words
Nothing, really.

When the personal asserts itself
As the dominant truth

We can be assured
A larger subjectivity will bubble up

Within Being – Being,
Which is the Common.

One might finally discover what
Bodies and minds are capable of!

Neighborhoods devoted to
Love of the other, where neighbor

Means stranger and
Stranger means lover

Like downtown once
Presumably was

During the glory days of Movement X
Or Coterie Y, its mysterious linguistic

No isolate self
Gathering dead wood on a cliff.

6

The loom of the rain
Weaves adoration with sorrow

And loom of the snow
Since suddenly big flakes.

Now-again sensitive to the trace
Death leaves on self-definition.

To almost-images of
Sap and ancestral fire.

Too little bits of
Present moment

That won't exact revenge
For having once been lived

And stay sane for the sake
Of soaking up available sunlight

Things solid yet
Beyond resemblance

Kisses on the mouth
On an empty road.

How a digression
Practically becomes political

If it breaks away a bit
From the feeling of unease

That was the main line
Of the original argument.

Hermitage
In the fragile.

7

One, the top of which
Blown off

By its own vol-
Canic force.

The other, tumescent.
A hidden cleft.

Automobility no guarantee of
Getting anywhere: in fact just the opposite

Is probably true, and height
And depth so much road-kill.

We are pancake people, according to
Richard Foreman, zombies in our cars...

Only a mountain
With its plunge and swoop

Might reveal
The revitalizing spark.

That tarnished logs burn
Bright once ignited is also

Crucial, all imperfections
And dirt finally incidental.

Deep aggregates break apart
In our digestive crucibles

And make us forget our theorizing
Even as we see the substance of the theory

Like a shimmering
Red web emerge before our eyes.

Some mists rise
For the express reason

There is another
Side of the river

But the majority of roads are
Maladjusted to our coming:

The body
Is a dangerous thing.

Flight impossible and besides
This is not the kind of suffering

One could flee from.
That even harmony would lessen.

We hear a gallows tuba let us
Have it with its deep pops of sound.

The movements of the wood
Are subtle, because a tree.

8

The present and the
Absent just as voice

Is produced from inside
The body and of course

The body is produced
By other absent bodies

And the mind is carved
On a dangerous ledge

On the wall of a cave
At the axis of our enthusiasms.

South face of
The soft mountain

Sometimes reachable
With one's hands as from

A distance one does not
See the mountain chain.

Or perhaps sights only
The two tallest peaks

One intact,
One broken.

How decide
What is necessary?

I have come to this cliff
Multiple times already and

It is always different
Save quarry and raven

And the relation of the aura
To the soles of one's feet.

Most times in fact one can't even see
The mountains for the doubts.

— I'm no good at being
Fatalistic but I suspect

Such facts do
Influence our form.

9

Dawn
A lifetime away.

An other face forms
A ford over the invisible

And I'm not
Making it across.

Face that
Is naked, a lyric

Stretched taut
Between speech

And silence,
Apparently erased.

When eyelids refuse to bend
To the surpassing wave

That makes each of us organic
And curved.

Up on that cliff
Splitting wood in the inexplicable

Yes, I wish I were gathering
Dead wood on a cliff

In exertion or awe of
The forces that drive us

In the mist, in the shroud
Of the clouds and the cold.

Too lost in narrow exhaustion
Now to focus and gaze.

Inescapable
Unless the mind rests

In the larger uprising of
Eyelids finally

Finally bent
In submission.

The naked face contorts
In its cage of discontent.

And would be beautiful
If one could see it.

10

Daylight breaks
Across broad trunks.

Amid glistening waves
Sudden, indefinable drizzle.

The visible trembles
And possibly dissolves

Since an open
Free-floating term

Vivid shorthand
For a process called

Reverberation,
Called call, called response.

As the setting down of new codes
Compels us to repair ever deeper

Into the forest of language
"The sun rises from vapor

And sets in ice"
Nowhere and never.

The immediate emotion is
A person jumping out of her skin.

The poem is
The skin she jumps into?

Too much fragmentation would mean
Each piece is received

Homogenously, without context,
Which betrays the very theory

Of the fragment: too much
Continuity closes the poem down.

Not to remember anymore what one did
The day before, what was that conversation,

Why sublimate the key in one's hand
And the lock it fits?

Wild storms, their lightning
And thunder, grow more

And more distant
In the distractions of time.

No further chance of being seduced by
Acres and acres of tempting amplitude?

A clarinet leads in to a human voice,
Suggests to us an emotion that mingles

Masterful extremes
In a single phrase.

11

A rock detached from
The rest of The Earth
And thrown into outer space

Could not be more forlorn
Than the plastic chair tossed,
Now planted, on the highway divider.

Whizz! The poet
And the environmentalist
End up attorneys for the bird

Or wolf pack or oily sea.
And *lexopoesis*, law-making,
Is a legitimate human activity:

Depending what laws the agents pass
It will be either sunny or cloudy,
Unseasonably hot, unusually salty.

As for last month's ice storm —
Branches and trunks avalanched
In splintered pieces

The spectacle of all that
Arboreal pain
Suddenly political...

A grain of tumult on the otherwise
Bland and sandy shore is complicit
With the universal

Or the ocean as the universal,
The universe that refuses to let
A specific wave return in a timely way

To the rest of the sea, arranging
For its stay where there should be land,
Turncoat against the stable and dry.

So a poem is only as good
As it sources, intoxicants
And air, angel wrestling muse

Wrestling *duende*, impressions
A brain stores becoming plural
In a city or forest lending us its vortex.

No clutter in
Minds committed to each particular as
Naming each obligates the mind to leap

Into abstraction,
The parts of what we know that we cannot
Possibly see. Some few shreds of what

Must have once been a giant
Octopus, pink and suckered,
Arrange themselves on the pebbly beach.

12

Debussy spoke of
An inaudible musical object

Every composition strives
To suggest the presence of.

Bronk suggests light does not exist
To illuminate the objects:

Objects exist
To demonstrate light's

Range — hues —
Textures.

What is the likelihood
That bright stand of alder bordering

Bank of America's parking lot
Will still be standing next year?

That I will be standing nearby
To check the transformations?

That the Bank of America
And its checks will still be

Valid,
The parking lot a parking lot

Or the whole space reclaimed
By alders and their kin

On the basis of
Which apocalypse?

The human abstract mixes well
With chanterelles

Just loosened
From the soil

And even the "I'
Partakes

In the charm of things
If one realizes

We too have mycelia
That trail underground for miles.

In a dark age
We live in monasteries.

HEAVY SUBLIMATION

Waves lap against the rock.

Smooth stone to the smoothness of themselves.

Give themselves to land.

Rock gives way, slightly.

As if overwhelmed by pleasure in itself the next wave swamps the little shore and itself in its own blonde froth.

A new wave arches in from a particularly lewd angle, softly crashing onto the expectant, hardened form that awaits it.

Pinkness as of tongue invites the mind to wonder

what skin is for   wave heavier than the rock it lifts

rock   lifts

is spilled   dissipates to sand.

Such dark smiles, neither friendly nor automatic.

The next wave seems to perspire
as it warms the overturned earth it engulfs and disperses.

This encounter between ocean and shore
goes on all night

Into the morning.

As waves drain away the shore's strength.
Reach afternoon.

And the approach of new night.

Still, the shore pleads to be emptied.

So we locate our bodies in relation to bodies folding over us.

Because of libido two things always have some relation to one another,
each active, each passive, in its own way, in different moments and
moods.

The next thing over to naked
Intimacy occurs in public when wall and vine refuse to become
undraped.

If the world is unfinished it is because bodies cannot resolve to become
either organisms or elements, living beings or inanimate energies.

Desire raises havoc when a tease too far provokes the dwarf in us to overreact and renounce love, reify the yonic as other than itself.

Touch is both glorification and chore.

Pantomiming pleasure
Wind strokes the teeming limbs   tree
    barely even barked.

Soft trunk, limbs bending in the breeze,
grazed against by an invisible being.

When the speaking voice sings the organic body speaks...

Tree thick with foliage   plunging downwards
as if to crush the wet animal crouched at its base ...
the landing is soft   pulp meets pulp
the animal lost in the splay of tree   is not hurt.

Slender and tall, drawing the eye upward,
darkening earth and sky,
a wave cracks against the unprotected face.

Dark, dark as mud and burnt fruit, yet bursting with sap,
dark, dark sapling, so young, bowled in the back,
bending over a soaking mammal lost in the storm,
laughing as it strokes the mammal's haunch.

A slit in a tree, proximity to which provokes convulsions in the pebbles arrayed before it.

      Arched and cool an alder leans back
          And is admired.

After the braided wave hits the bather,
dissolving in froth while the bather flounders in the foam,
the bather regains his feet, stammering, gasping for air,
looking in all directions:
a child is alone and incomplete, just like everyone else.

Released from sickness, from isolation, from individualism, from the tissue of a name.

This shore that traps all drives and submits them to intensification.

      Not fusion but display, wind in the branches.

Things jut up through which water washes, over millennia smoothing the gargantuan tines of unspeakable formations.

"How long have I known you?" whispers the wave
to the King of the Sand Castle.
He, in no condition to reply.
Nights are dark and sultry and filled with sound.

"You want me?" intones the alder to the breeze that seeks to embrace it,
the tree intoxicated but firm, flexible but unimpressed.

26

Two pairs of lips held close but not touching.
One affects the other, one feels the other a rip in the fabric.

A wall expands to meet one's face, block one's view,
even as two bodies meet, because the other body is that wall.

The roots of trees burst apart the pavement, rendering the path
        treacherous,
enraged, like that famous frozen sea suddenly welling up.

    We are enthralled as the boat is drawn down, into the eels,
off the coast.

Stripping as for a swim in the blatant ocean, the ocean smiling obscenely
  at one's efforts to be completely submerged.

    Stop fighting, both of you, for both of you are right.

LIKE ACHILLES' SHIELD

Tiny cabin
Improbable among crags

So high up
The Pacific can't be heard

And a bird call almost
Abstract in its elevation.

Look, the ocean glistens, apparently
Flat, signifying calm.

Yet for the overdosed
(And the aged) even a pond

Or puddle can be dangerous
Should one slip in the evening

When no one is around
When a dip in temperature

Will lead to
Hypothermia

And water to
Literal drowning.

Between the drug house and her
Parent's home, the young woman —

Having insisted on departing wasted
Through woods and twilight mist —

Encounters a pond or puddle, meth-
Amphetamines twisting through her mind.

The final instants of a world.
A storm in the brain out of control.

The pond
A seeming torrent.

So a rural paradise
Becomes hell

For the parents
Who survive her

And their home,
Which provided no protection

Against the drug,
Forever now a harrowing.

A pond? A puddle.
From earliest stories

A puddle snores
In its isolation from the flow

Except as it perhaps
Imperceptibly seeps.

Or else it
Evaporates, like a life.

(Factitious ghosts
Fill an organism

Without scruple
Or delay

Like downpour
In a trench.)

If water, which flows
Lower, ever lower,

Knows no end
To its descent...

If the present is
The eye of a God,

The past is God's
Digestive tract and bowels,

And the future,
The future, the future is damp...

Such fine handiwork
Went into that shield's crafting!

The blazing images, the ply work
Fretted into its defensive build.

And all of it useless,
Completely useless

For protecting one's child
From her singular death, by

Overdose, hypothermia,
Drowning.

Water crashes against a brow,
Puddles over...

Olympian thoughts
Emit from a tiny cabin

Among improbable crags,
Champion a certain detachment

The placidity of the
Ocean, the abstraction of the bird...

PROLOGUE AND EPILOGUE

Prologue and Epilogue are two moons circling
The same planet, one that has not yet been named
Or even discovered. We only know of these moons
Because my mother the astronomer said they exist.

Prologue has a highly permissive atmosphere.
As on our moon, one can practically float through space.
Unlike our moon, Prologue has plenty of air to breathe.
The feeling on Prologue is one could end up anywhere.

Epilogue is deeply furrowed and rife with consequence.
It is known to be bone dry and it is thought
That very little moves on this moon, not even dust.
Yet its profile leaves room for some possibility of continuity.

Prologue and Epilogue orbit around their planet at different rates.
Prologue is much faster, as you might expect. It circles
Planet Unknowable at three times the rate of the other one.
Nevertheless Epilogue too finally makes it all the way around.

How is it astronomers like my mother know so much about
These two moons, and so little about the planet they orbit?
Maybe it has to do with all that "from womb to tomb" folderol?
Or is there a good astronomical explanation for this unusual mystery?

POETRY AS EXPLANATION #1

Because a face that provokes longing, overwhelming
Longing, sometimes expresses comical alarm.

Because less *retentia* would mean less
Everything that shines later, in the refining.

Desire's tension dissipates into the acceptance
Of impossibility: that very same tension

Strung just as tightly in place
The next morning, just because.

Because very young, and very small,
And trying to cross a four-lane street.

Because from the carillon the mother's promise,
City view stretching to forever, optimism's peal.

Because *Creature Feature* had its transcendent charms,
No preacher ever needed, Saturday morning

Rituals of *monstrum* and amazement. Because
Communities are now footnotes to the highway...

Death on the roads, ghouls wrapped in gauze
As seen from the rear-view mirrors of women's cars.

Because storm shutters shred in my arms
I must be the storm: or because the particles

In the shutters in the act of shredding refuse to
Defend any longer against the thundering roar

They must be the storm's conductors.
Because one loves whom one should not love.

Because in the troubled loam
Stands a shock of trees, trembling with mice.

Because it was the last house of its kind to be built
For a great many centuries, one that

At its inaugural, after the incantation,
Drew down a spectral fire that burned up

Not only the offerings made at its altar
But the entire temple, inside and out.

Because that house filled with the glory
Of its principle of composition.

Because of texting
At risk on the road: youngsters,

Friends, writing as they drive.
Because some breakfast cereals

Are invitingly open and round,
Similar to the possible:

Twelve year old girl falls 180 feet
Down a fourteen story

Chimney, is cushioned by soot
In the basement

Incinerator, where she is found
Alive, because of those ashes.

POETRY AS EXPLANATION # 2

Because the known is dipped
In the ink of the unknowable.
Because inklings of the unknowable
Show up in language.
Because blood sometimes is granted vision,
Gushes out in torrents, enthusiastically,
As if to see the sights.
Because the pebble of the person
Teeters even on solid ground.
Because our age is the marsupial dawn
As certain old poets happily
Exclaim, at the very beginning of
What we purpose to want to know.
Because the "I" can never be institutionalized
Entirely, no matter which school
Or residence or group home or enclosure
Is invented for its comfort or edification.
Because consciousness is empty and free.
Because Nature is a frame
One could also call
An eel.
Because in mid-flight
Falcon seized jay and
I'm the jay and the gyre.
Because the power snaps off
With the ease of a bikini top.
Because just a step away exist

Regions of darkness more archaic
Than earth itself.
Because one so easily becomes another
At certain junctures in the work
That one comes to question
The meaning of the = sign.
Because we proposed a plan for the reform
Of the dictionary: to arrange the thing
Chronologically, by birth date of each word.
Because in an English language dictionary
The first word would of course be imagine
A convertible hidden in a bamboo forest
And two people in the convertible, making out.
Because water drips from a spigot and
Below rushes through a ravine and
Mists plying the woods are as free
In their movement as a conversation
Though perhaps not as necessary
As the primary monologue of the water.
Because of a glade where rapture intensifies
The longer we listen to the marching brook.
Because water collects in tin cans, beer bottles, barrels,
Jugs, flower vases, tanks, tubs, storm drains,
Catch basins, the holes in rocks.
Because like WCW
I want to see the unknown shine, like a sunrise.
Because energies organize in a single wave
And disperse just as suddenly.
The moon rises, a ripe *oro blanco,* just because.

Because according to the lead investigative detective
Actions speak louder than French.
Because as he reads aloud the poem
The features of the ill poet's face
Light up like a lantern:
When the reading is over
His face goes dim, baffled, as if by
His death, for which he is only partially prepared.

POETRY AS EXPLANATION #3

Because amplitudes awaken in last light of day
Final instants linger in sashes of purple or pink.
Because of the intact body of a fallen fir
Whose vast root system splays towards the sky,
Lifting up huge clods of soil as if on display.
The world enters us, scooping out
Distinctions, forging in us
Necessary artificialities we also must fight
Because we want to differentiate further.
Because only if luminescent roots
Establish themselves in the soils of the unconscious
Could one finally do something radical
Down there in the poem
Amidst fungi and decayed
Literatures, nutrients, souls.
Because inorganic and organic
Connect in the stone.
Because in both natality and death
One is as immobile as a tree,
Compared to the worms so febrile
And quick to receive the latest prize.
Because impeccable solitude encloses desire,
The underneath of underneath body
A dark, intractable dance,
The root's display in the aether.
For a person to die means to be buried:
For a tree to die means to be unburied:

Because people and trees are different.
Because every domestic situation
Is at the same time foreign
And beyond comprehension.
Because after the *aristae* of this
Comes the *aristae* of that, like
The day the lectern caught the light
And suddenly, rather than an empty
Shell, seemed of itself to speak
From the center of a distinct wood.
The immediate limitation of the individual
Is another individual, making demands,
Because we are "social" beings in our essence.
Because the heart is a poor island
If the light and colors of the libidinal landscape
Do not modify its bitter reds.
Because a blonde raven, not driven by rules
She can obey or even recognize
Disrupts the color in everything else.
The *aristae* of an object, say a red pear
On a marble counter, comes as a surprise
Because there can be no representation of the way
We are fragments of some larger body.
Or else one inflates to the size of a dirigible
Because of over-the-top pronouncements.

POETRY AS EXPLANATION #4

Because moss is a sea overtaking sentient trees,
Older than them by far and
Lapping at their branches,
Dangling downward like necklaces of green salt.
Because those trees are already ghostly
And offer no opinion:
From the ridge one sees thousands wave,
Slaves leading secret lives
In the vibration of the visible.

Because three fishermen shift their net,
Hoping to catch more than
Personal circumstance
And because for all the fine speaking
Fleeting is not the same as fluid.
Because out of a vast freezer recently disabled
A new ocean pours into the old
And an armada of fresh indignities
Plague the wannabe dominant species.

Because rock and fire at work in the water
Invigorate a breaker rolling towards me.
Because the air is knocked from my trunk
And I come up agog, gasping for
Thought. Because the contingency of
The contingent a constant
Impossibility for thinking,

Whose representations make
The thing seem like it had to be.

Because other signals are being sent
To some other sense I can't say.
Mushrooms soil the mouth and like
The worms we savor that, just because.
Because through thick foliage I observe
The eye of a deer, opened
Unnaturally wide, and then wider,
No other part of the creature visible.
Because apricot grappa
Diffuses into the furthest
Taste buds of one's palette.
Because there can be
No representation of the way we are
Perspiration of some larger body.

Because of the grief of the gash,
Its power to make us bow, oysters
In limbo, paddle plunging into
Flowering brine, limbic beds of
Oysters, winged, winged salt.
And because of words and forms
That outlive what they refer to.

POETRY AS EXPLANATION #5

Because fluted bark and pyramidal crown
Flash in the sunlight.
Because time is no mere chronology
And the body politic is subject
To unpredictable whims, even as
Activities of daily life are arranged
In assemblages of increasingly
Integrative power. Nature, a juggler
Adept with many balls and torches,
So vast we take a big chance daring
To interfere with its performance
(Since we are also one of its props)
Also too is not linear: because of that
In a dim zone of memory giant
Extinct fireflies blink (each
Firefly the size of a dinner plate).
Passing from the finite to the infinite
Because we must, is, practically speaking,
Impossible, while down the hill the dead trees
Gathered by a more proximate heat
Are turned into charcoal in a matter of hours.
The ruins of an orchard which
On closer inspection are revealed to still yield
Fruit, because it is the fences that are down and
The human hand that would guide the orchard
That is missing...
Because Love's half-life is less than radium's

Yet feels as if its fuel will never be spent.

Because we live in the gap

Between the finite

And its opposite number, which

Isn't a number at all,

Careening wherever, whenever

We are hungry for food,

Desirous and without career.

Because "it's raining" and "I'm wet"

Is no more than a difference in perspective,

Depending on one's condition of shelter...

Because the Actual contains both

Inwardness and physical extension

While the Possible offers

Only the former or, possibly,

Only the latter: by some magic of the

Near-at-hand substance

Learns inwardness, actuality begins.

Because the earth is now loud with human

Life, while the flight of an owl is silent.

Like the look of recognition on the face

Of a one year old, after a parent's

Three week absence: because suddenly

That other, the one the child hadn't even noticed

Was missing, has been completely restored.

POETRY AS EXPLANATION # 6

Because icebergs
The unconscious crashes into
Calve, eventually joining
The unconscious.

Because half of what I was before I fell
To the half of you turned away from me
Stirs us both into recollecting
We are again in the underground
Of some transitional phase,
Never to coincide, compensated
For not participating in
The myth of the other half
By something we cannot name
But that is also definitely mythic.

After the latest face-to-face,
Serene: a day later the hallowed
Anguish returns even stronger,
Because...
Because the will to live protrudes from
The need to destroy oneself in love.
Because from salt sea
Appearance itself appeared
And the gaze of the lover
Fell upon the beloved:
They were now indeed

Two parts. And because they are
Apart, rapture becomes a kind of
Citadel, tidal processes suddenly
Demonstrate awkward constraint.

Because a voice throws off boulders
I so much want to ask the one with the voice
What I am going to become.
Because it burns in the tiny infinite.
Because so little of what we are
Makes it over into the finite expanse of day.
Because this is no lifeless abstraction
Though maybe a novelist could be
Even more concrete concerning
Rituals rooted in circumstance,
Formica kitchen counter, frozen steak.
Axes are good for cutting up creation,
Sledges and mauls for splitting it:
Axe that is deliberately incomplete,
Just because it is deliberately incomplete...
But even a bony arm ends in a fist.

A shared solitude translates into remembering
Nothing, because...because...
Because all the evidence for
The need to speak
Is there in our speech.
Because I didn't feel like reading for almost
A year, and then I felt like I wanted to do
Nothing but read for almost two years after that.

POETRY AS EXPLANATION #7

Because of the
Unhappiness of a potted hydrangea
Fluffed up with no place
To become
Hurriedly, I
Left the café.
Because the poet stepped out
Onto the stage, and found
No stage, no audience,
Neither desk, notebook,
Pen, or laptop, and because
As the poet fell, the poet
Sensed there still might be
A language, that even if
The abyss of the creaturely
Is inchoate, also too it is
Agog with names...
Because there is a rhythm
To your face
And that rhythm is the ruler.
Because the eye contact is divine.
Because to have a position in time
I must be a fact...
And I'm not.
Because a body isn't
The same as a fact,
Nor consciousness in its throes.

Because of an immense space
As alluring to words
As it is impenetrable, aloof...
Because, in synopsis,
No stone is terminal (Lorca).
Because of her expression,
So suffused with suffering
In ways one is forbidden to
Soothe, even should one
Have the spine.
Because walking on the beach
Feet encounter jagged objects.
Because *the body is the plot.*
Because a voice without a body
Summoned a voice in a body
To carry an ominous message
To another city, demonstrating that
Being is full of surprises
Such that a being with a body
Is likely to lie awake
In the belly of a fish, crying out
Over its situation for hours.
Because one's mouth a moth
Wanting to reach
The surface of the moon.

POETRY AS EXPLANATION #8

Because amidst
This sultriness
I dream of becoming
A bead of perspiration
Clinging to a cinnamon throat.
Because the body
Interprets the voices of pebbles
And of parapets, otherwise
One fails to remain pliable.
Because I stand by a fountain,
There the waters power up
Like a moving hill
And all is sound.
Because Image cross-hatches
Sensation and Idea,
Unions we cannot decode
Without the participating units
Drifting off, disaffected.
Because our soil
Is sadness, which
Perfumes solitude
Without relieving the worst of it
While the drizzle of vision
Threatens to turn into a downpour.
Because to be taken by the wind:
To be taken: to be nothing
But my guess at the other's next whim.

Because I should have clowned more
On the brink of the voluptuous:
What if thinking never arrives
At necessity but composition
Can, just not right now?
The featherweight universe
Is suddenly leaden
Because I let speech get deadened,
The ground of language so stressed
It gives migraines to the stars.
Still we speak into the receivers
Of smart phones because
We trust that somewhere inside the technology
Lurks the human voice.
Because
The last time we spoke, in person,
Close to midnight,
You looked and sounded like a goddess of doom.
Because parting is such sweet
Division of labor, I mean parting
The waters so that a single tribe
Might pass through, and it takes all night
To get the thing to work,
A condition we know will last for only
A few miraculous seconds, the Red Sea
In the retelling, on the verge of
Swallowing up the VIPS's as well.
Because a desirable incandescence,
Of which there can be no doubt.

POETRY AS EXPLANATION #9

Because each branch of the tree
Tries to memorize the trunk.
Because I fail, and fall,
Solemnly you watch my life sever.
Because of a spear in such constant use
We can't possibly be breathing.
Because the heart's desire to be faithful
To the infinity of love
Programs an impossible colossus.
Because insomnias of the dead
Keep the books read, the writing
At work, reflection bellicose.
Because dread of the next word
Is an emotion without name.
Unparaphrasable endeavor of the worldly:
Because each act is free, hence causeless.
Because children climbing on rocks exercise
Their rights, material, efficient, formal and final.
Because from outlaw to classic to formal logic
To burning branch to *acte gratuit*
The exquisite jam of poets covers everything.
Because thunder and lightning,
Smoking mountain, blaring trumpet:
Who wouldn't be terrified, who wouldn't
Want an intermediary to go over there
And do the talking for us, even if one knows
One should go and have a look for oneself,

Reckon with what is being done in one's name,
The power that both blasts and beckons,
A series of miracles, a sequence of threats?
Because large stones sometimes
Sing with such surprising softness.
Because after Daphne
The laurel tree in-dwells.
Because to be left by someone
Is to be left by everyone, even if
It turns out it was merely a delay.
Because all ego all the time:
You give us 22 minutes,
We'll give you the world.
Because all id all the time:
You give us 22 minutes
We'll give you the real.
Because if one weighs these words
Fairly, one hears the ocean.
Because everything we write
Is first person, and first person
Is always impersonal.

POETRY AS EXPLANATION #10

Core samplings of language
Collect in a book —
That dangerous crawl space —
Because the book
Dissimulates the archaic
Much as dream does.
Because silent and isolate
Distance is our name,
Aura, aura-sphere,
Word-event, mothers
We hold the hands of,
Looking up.
Because a caress
Activates a view of objects.
Because a thought returns
From a summons bathed
In the beauty that summoned it.
Because individual consciousness
Confronts its limit, an unlit candle
Blinking from the cupboard nook.
Because the image of an image
Frees the thing, no?
Because color flees,
Dispersing into many forms,
Fleck of red hidden in a cat's fur,
Gold, diasporic, lodged in the wing
Of mysterious bird #1

Flying over Glacier #2, sunlit.

Because dream is stronger than experience

And is the work we are lost in.

Damn it, time opens up

Like a bottomless ravine

Because there is no feasible plan

For our next conversation.

Because noon cuts the dewy morning

Down to sober, but desire fights back

In the form of a fruit

Shooting its juice at the sun

Through ripped covers of its own bright skin.

Because it is my place to praise you

And thereby to risk imminent death.

Because trinkets of speech

Suddenly become treasures.

Because of the city's best

Fruit-stand, moonlit, nearly two

In the morning, mangos piled high

From Mexico, Haiti,

Several other lands.

Because so deeply immersed in one's happiness

It takes months to pass to even become

Partly aware of it.

Because the feeling of elsewhere

Is a quiet joy.

Because persuasion

Is as slender as a vine-maple,

As weak as water.

Because we should only examine

The confused, combinatory state

In a confused, combinatory state.

Because there *will be* a next conversation...

POETRY AS EXPLANATION #11

Because a particular clearing
Surrounded by particular cedars
Is blessed with a particular receptivity
To another, only vaguely
Particular world.
Because that other world
Suddenly comes into earshot,
Pleading for someone to speak it.
Feed the torch
The moral fuel,
Burn it entirely,
Like cedar burning,
The poison, the remedy, because...
Because we are not on the side of forts
Or walls but doorways,
Rooftops, hinges, holes.
Between accident and substance
Loom auto-suggestively induced
Mountains, to be crossed:
We embark, but because
Some can't be descended
We are obliged to live in the heights.
In each individual, laughter
Awaits the moment it might erupt
Because every break-up of equilibrium
Presents a cure for what we caused
In our more serious moments.

Because mischief is thus partly moral
But mostly mischievous, and if you
Answer with anger you run the risk
Of causing the mystery to scatter
Like a flock of geese, ungainly
In their take-off. Because of a
Hesitation between sound and sense.
Because bursting with poppy and recollection.
Because of a spring of water turned to stone
Yet still subliminally coursing,
Coursing, moving rocks lubricated
By hidden beads of moisture.
Because distress too scents the air
From several miles off, frantic spoor
In eco-systems of care. Because
Magic doesn't always require ritual:
Luminous sobs, bodies at a distance,
Lairs of the nutriment. Because
A unique openness of her eyes
Survives the death of God
Contact with them wrings from me
Another round of spiritual turmoil.
Because clear, rushing stream-water,
Transparent and satirical, ribbing
The stones, no longer seems possible.

POETRY AS EXPLANATION #12

From dark abyss
To celestial splendor
Without GPS
Or system of prayer:
A sheet
Covers a bed
And crackles, just because.

Because the sight of a face
Surpassing description
Surpasses description...
As if philosophy alone
Could bespeak the face as face
Without representing what is,
Hence, without losing what it is:
(See Poe's "The Oval Portrait"):
(See philosophy as a form of speech):
(See the philosopher, her face lit by
Café Minerva's candle light, lamp
Light, light thrown from the laptop
On which she wants to write.)

Because in the silence of writing
The sober in a split second
Becomes my ecstatic calm.
Because across the table
Minutes later her expression reveals

Unalloyed anguish – sudden,
Harsh, and caused by *writing itself.*

Because the infinite is always unassimilated...
Suffering-in-writing.
Because to relieve her *Suffering-in-writing*
Is why I am here, supposedly.
When I note: she is humming.
Because causation is, according to Hume,
"The cement of the universe."
Because that which flows before cement's
Invention, and comes again after its demise...
Because love calls into us
And challenges the core...

As a droplet
Hangs from the faucet
Never falling,
The face, in defeat,
Does not succumb
To its defeatism,
And, in the end,
Disorders all.

VARIATIONS ON SANE

Invisible traumas
Surface visibly
In black of night

Wounds, recurrences,
Transmitted materially
One psyche to the next.

A successful revolution
Might yet happen tomorrow
So it's important to imagine

The respective donning of masks:
At its root the real is both genders,
Wanting the female above all else.

It is also true every amorous *system* is enemy
To the desiring grain of the senses
As when deep snow melts

And you can see the impact
Winter made on the supporting ground.
No one can live without such complexity

Yet chance is the original form of communication
And sometimes provides one with a condor's quill.
Wonders wander into the range of the possible...

*

What cries out in whistling anguish
From the twigs
Deepens now in the roar of logs.

Roof's
Roots
Routed any moment now

Though all
Remains quite orderly
On the surface.

Or an eagle's wing
Tumbling from
Its bedraggled corpse.

I pick up the wing —
Huge —
And struggle to carry it

From the body
The rest of the course.
I am a woman

Following a man
Into a mostly
Darkened cave...

*

Everyday life
Is a place
Beyond prayer

Non-brain, non-God
Somehow making its way
Into ecstatic phonemes.

The blood on a pear
Attests to the simplest havoc:
This violent omnipresent.

Were those large raptors
Or Chinese kites way up there
In the city's cauterizing smog,

On the verge of kissing?
The way up and the way down
May well be one

But only the caws
Of crows
Penetrate my present window.

I don't want to go
Away! But rain washes
Everything into the distance.

*

Writing from the darkness
Frogs in chorus creak
And are some guidance.

Elk antlers
Gleam in a puddle,
Reminders of a former age.

Firs, ferns, amanitas,
A thousand-and-one mosses
Conquer highways

In a matter of days,
Return us to that older era.
OK with me

Since speech itself
Is dependent upon moisture
Sprung from woodland panic.

Elation fades as the imagined message
Subsides into the absence of
Any message at all...

Were I not so down tonight
I'd have the moon
To myself.

*

The heart is fascist
When stonewalled by
The object of its love

And a flame advancing
Along the meridian
Is the true berserker

Claiming all
The highways and their traffic,
Until the madness seems to burn out.

Some crow, seething, stares at me
From the side of a country road:
I've interrupted him in the act

Of killing
A garter snake,
Intervening instinctively

On the side of the snake.
The snake leapt at me then, harmless.
The crow's beak had left a hole in its head.

The shadow of the ocean
Only becomes visible to the visitor
Who approaches it from a certain angle.

*

The moon is in my beverage.
Or, in not burning my tongue,
Some flame just as subtle.

The moon, even at its coolest
Suggests some encounter just down
The road (another crow-and-snake?)

But no, in this drama
The moon is a white van
Parked on the sidelines of what happens.

Because in this drama there is a woman
Who can no longer make out the trees
From the blizzard of her trauma.

Heartbroken in neck
Heartbroken in knees
Heartbroken in sensorium:

Hot springs sprung
From a giantess's tears
Unending.

Snowy Lake unfrozen,
Fresh and clear
As the marten drinks.

*

What if the brain is a bone
And the mind is the meat on the bone
Or rather the flesh that joins to other flesh

Ardor, seeking, suckle of
Milk, when philosophical poetry
Stops arguing and becomes song.

The lyric is the part of the argument
That is oblivious to being part of anything.
Its modality, so slim, lights up

The contradiction. Then through the dazzle
To glimpse another's pain but only to
Want to shield the self from it

And the lyric dissolves:
Impossible to protect against
Another person's unconscious.

In this drama a woman
No longer can make out the trees
From the blizzard of her trauma.

Her rape repeats itself
And repeats itself
In gusts of fear and rage

As if sleep's deepest thought
Were always this excruciating violation,
Its ingrown wrath.

And upon waking each flashback claim
Necessitates a trip to the hospital
Where they bring out the kit

And, senile, past seventy, she swears her nightmare
Is true... each time they test for it
Negatively: each time, for her, it is true.

Approaching a broken branch,
Identifying.
Its posture on the ground

Practically fetal. At my desk
The tinkle of incoming
E-mail, some of them insane...

*

Hiding out
In the position
All things are appearances.

A truck is said to jack-knife.
After that, flocks of ibis vanish
As well as all other signs of life.

Like a tree that loses every last branch
And ends up a trunk, crashing
In angry surf against others of its kind.

An obscurity from which
Clarity begins to wriggle free
A clarity that glows from within

Darkest burning coal
A tractor crashing through a fence
Running over a bonsai tree

The master had accidentally
Left out there,
In the open.

Vague friendship with a seemingly
Happy couple, nodding and gesturing
To one another in the web of the familiar.

A giant raises the beach to his lips.
It is the sea he is after,
Not the sand, not the people...

*

Not to reify the very collectivity of the living
The practice of thought is supposed to emancipate
But aren't we all non-self-identical?

No alienating mechanism can insure
Intellectual audacity
But it can help us stop making objects

Folks will fear and worship.
However there really is a whirlpool
In these parts, grasping claws

Along Scylla's channel and
The ridge with the sheer drop
Insures we will experience

Parts of our body as not there –
The heart, for example,
And the brain.

Make-believe is
Light-hearted,
Desire feral

And the dead
Are the majority.
But they don't

Have smart phones,
Only rarely
Respond to letters or cards.

*

Infinity, interrupted
By a blossom-drenched breeze
That must have been

The true infinite, no?
A delirium that leaves
No trace but interruption.

You hand me
An apricot-sized fruit
That is most likely an apricot.

The amorous world makes contact
With the conservative world

And is killed by it, makes contact
With the liberal, and is killed again.

In its next rebirth the amorous seeks
No world but itself – and dies, forever.

A NEW VENICE

What light
Is left
Is dark water
Running in
Deepest silence,
Under the words.
We try to write:
One tries to write:
You seem to be writing:
I'm writing now, of
Light and water.
Or we speak of how
Slowly sinking Venice is currently
Model for the world, all the
Oceans enlarging, lands
Awash in seas, human made
Warming so hard at work.
So that Venice,
The way they build there,
Is our only hope.
Venus always was our only hope,
And now the science proves it.
Dew and spark rise from
Darkly gathering salty waters.
There is only beauty.
A bug dies of love.

Doom clenches my throat.

One knows only desire for a particular.

UNDER THE OCULUS

Enough sky obscured
So sky gods can be seen:

The idea of the eye
Realized architecturally

Produces a solar space
Of solace and concentration.

By the oculus of language
Vision musters versions:

It is a happy thing that consciousness
Is non-self-identical

Small spaces opening between
Ample clouds

Sky, earth, and body
Timidly intimating a particular

Desire to intertwine
From the vantage of their difference.

The lovers glimpse each other,
One of them cries.

The lovers clash:
One of them gives.

The lovers need hide
In thickets, rain forests

Offices. Oh,
But divinities do die when

Episteme denies them
Their ambrosia and ichor:

Episteme dies when
Divinity wills it:

Death becomes rosy
In gardens of the incarnate.

A particular crow caws:
The sky opens even wider.

Sunlight, atmospheric
Blue, heaven's hue,

The lovers dividing cleanly
Into the one who wounds

And the one
Who is wounded.

One of the lovers commands:
The other *doesn't* obey:

The ensuing action more deeply
Surrendered than any obedience.

If I am to be worthy of a love
That turns into worship

My only hope is to plunge again
Deeply into the poem.

Locating past lives in another's gasps,
Breath's bud, tightened collar.

Rebirth: the expression of Utopian
Polarity in a world otherwise flat.

This mastiff was once a man,
Someone's husband it might be said.

Time itself is complicated
By the mind's designs

As hatched
In different eras:

Liberation and constraint,
A million times before.

Oh, the sun just came out
Someone says

In a rich
Southern accent.

Meanwhile the make out session
Goes on and on

Month after
Voluptuous month!

White sheet of a cloud
Now blocks the sun

Willing the eye to want to
Imagine what is behind it.

All that withheld blue,
All that blaze from Apollo.

Some kids in a church group
Enter the petit pantheon:

A girl sings Amazing Grace
Under the oculus.

Circle of sky provides relief
To minds in doubt.

Between desire and the desired
A walkway of lily pads

Light feet take easily
Except when one trips.

Or between desire and will
A deep shadow falls:

The shadow of pride.
The end of the ride?

No equality
Between the lovers.

Terrible, truly unconscionable.
Except, most of the time,

To the lovers themselves, doctrine
Betraying the truth it declares.

A coursing energy, always present
As feeling

And the god is lit
Unending, at the zenith.

A kind of sun that
Never gets around to setting.

RELEASED FROM WITHIN THE TURNED-UP CULTURES

Released from within the turned-up cultures
A toxin spreads through the body politic

Causing the imagination to cease to propagate
The imagination of even its barest condition.

Doomsday ads and hooligan optimism
Clog up the intersections and malls.

It is we who interrupt the progress, by "we"
I mean all these unaccounted-for graffiti and flyers.

So many suns the significant sun
Is lost in the glare

And where its torrent of light falls
Remains a mystery to you

And the whole of your Nation.
Fact blushes as crimson as fate.

Those of us who are present must not
Be afraid of the real and potential sorrows ...

She's seriously ill,
The parents know it now and

All quasi-certitudes about the future
Must be postponed.

A pillow for the head
Comes to represent

The apex of culture...
And its nadir.

Near a fir that glints
In a moment's sun

A strange animal is sighted
Dying into air.

And a ladder that relies
Largely on feel

When it comes to the question of
Where it should extend itself...

Each rung brightly beckoning
Once the decision is taken....

Seasonal rhythms obscure
The mineral joy of rushing water

Trackless waste of a world without consent
Consenting again to the kinetic.

Or the mind is
The most cosmopolitan region

Of the body
Except at the University of the Oblivious

Where Time's mask slips from off the face
Revealing an idiot grin

Biting down exactly on its own
Aspirations, self-esteem.

Your life weeps inside you for the falling rain.
A hermetic sack hardly seems credible.

"You will excuse my calling so late," she begins.
But her mind has atrophied, she says nothing further.

Social order sickened by a self-identification
That abandons all hope of its largest organ:

The skin, in shine, not in shine, in shine again,
Abed in reds and blues of our violent action.

MOSAIC FOR THE COURTSHIP OF TIME: A FICTION

1

A confused angel soars over
A cemetery, desecrated
The night before.
Indifferent jet, small grieving crowd:
Angel and distressed
Remain, at best, insects to one another.
Or a poet hopes the Lyric will compensate her
For exile from her country...
For the rupture with her family...
For the estrangement from the language
That very lyric stemmed from.
All that is left her is
A *duende* of the dismal,
Bobbing just above
The toppled head stones in
The cemetery the angel missed.

Or, after 58 years of marriage, she wakes up
    with no memory
Of her husband abed next to her,
Dementia creative of some recurrent demon
Named only "Who"?
So husband must court wife all over again
Each and every morning,
Each and every midnight.

That might be heaven.
Most times not so much.
Half plant half ghost, we humans.
The muse of the micro-second
Grows weaker each millisecond.
The living dead mushroom
In poisonous amanita bloom.
Who gave me gifts of confidence,
    of love —
Always at the proper distance
Between mother and child —
Might as well
    now be gone.
Or the artist decided to make a portrait of the deceased
Out of his own ashes: the deceased was her father.
And each art work she made after that —
Beeswax, birch coal, white marble dust
Mixed with the ashes of the person portrayed —
Gave a single individual their relative back
Visually, and by way of the writing it produced
In its wake, which the individual could read
    and be renewed by.
Out of absence springs a presence
That dissolves absence and presence
And leaves in its place...
And leaves in its place...

Or a mother created a forest in which to hide
The beings she loved.

Innumerable elements

And organisms without any single player

Taking the lead, not even water.

Morel, be my muse,

Until, as everything decays,

One can call formlessness form,

Not relentless breakdown and burn,

O forest that plays no favorites.

Or else the daughter lost herself in

The city of the immediate,

Which indeed does house a leader

On high in a tower,

Disembodied voices to direct its games,

Favorite overseer winners,

Special practices to conceal all morbidity.

Imminent chorus, stacking of stones:

Towers of glass, so many loans.

And she worshipped the sun in a thin figure of flesh,

A man who hardly seemed worthy of such worship

Except when he smiled?

More beautiful than Sita, saltier than Draupadi,

She gave her everything to that guy,

Barely worth the spine of a fish.

Why? She whispered:

"For the shape of his lips."

Owl by night, hawk by day: her prey

Advertises himself in the clearing

    and is happy

When caught, more lived and libidinized
    than a tabby.
A sound, and then another sound directed singly,
Invoking the flavor of love story and lordship.
Flame fluttering around flame that has drawn it
The five senses join, making a sixth, the five
Senses join, making a sixth, totaling twelve.
Then she's away, I'm away, a series
Comes to the end for the day.
And afterwards?

And the mother rejected her daughter
For not honoring the precepts.
Or a daughter watched
As her mother's
Body disintegrated
Before her very eyes.
Look, Mother's head
Lolling
    on her pillow.
A hospital bed:
The daughter can do little:
The daughter's husband
Completely useless
At the moment of his wife's despair.
Now what?
The theory of time
Belongs to the past,
The practice of time
To the present.
The future

Is bird song and nettles and
The mind her gift
To animal cry.
To the extent she remains unreachable
Our night is lit with stars.
From a tiny crab
Crawling from under a rock
To a galaxy
At the edge of the perceivable
Night exists
In front of our faces
And resists being seen.
Forest a mosaic of mineral
And life, except that each particle
Leaks into the other,
The artist explained in her talk.
Though she confessed afterwards
She could not conceive of
Her own death as mere
Leakage in the night.
Or, appreciative of the sky-light,
The wife grew concerned when
Its glass began to slide,
She asked her husband to fix it,
He didn't.
Or she was largely indifferent
To the alteration in their relations.
Or she flooded herself in anticipation
Of his return. Because

She was turned towards the coast:
The coast of what land mass, the coast
Of what consciousness, the coast of what cost
To feminine agency now demanded
By the latest shift in political power.
Or she knit a pink pussy cap and took
To the street, her highly trained voice
Joined with the others.
Or she studied carefully, very carefully
The arts and the sciences.
"I digress, and it makes me free,"
She wrote in her notebook.
On a more rueful note:
"As much as I want to be,
I am never alone."

2

If epic is a language of resistance
When, in *The Ramayana*,
Maricha, a kind of monster,
Says to Ravana , a worse monster,
"A king like you, of poor judgement
    and poor character,
A slave to his passions,
    takes bad advice
And, proposing the abduction of Sita,
Ends up destroying his kingdom,

His people, and himself,"
Then the reader on his smart phone
(Meaning reading about Trump)
Pays rapt attention,
Since Ravena did not.

Even fairy tale,
Usually thought of as cannibalized
By commodity,
Suddenly returns in the discourse,
Seemingly possible.
Shears, pitchforks,
Animated and at our command?
Three drops of berry juice?
The requirement to offer
Blood from our veins;
We cheat the devil and
Safeguard our souls
By ploy of the juice.
And the tools did come to life,
Assuming the form of an assemblage
Capable of obedience and motion,
Flight, cognition, and crime.
And the animated tools
Once they awoke
Begged us for work,
And stole things from far off
If we commanded it.

They needed the work;
Without it they would go crazy.
And we had plenty of assignments
With which to feed them.

One drop of rowan berry juice
From a rowan berry
Is one drop of rowan berry juice
From a rowan berry.
Two drops is two.
Three drops of rowan berry juice
From three rowan berries,
Offered propitiously,
Animates the metallic junk
Left in the lot, in the loft,
In the weeds by the market.
Pile of rods, be my robot.
Discarded tire, length of rope,
Rusting machete,
Assemble yourself
As ramshackle chariot.
When you are done doing that,
Kratt, get to work.
Be my wheeling hit man
But also my butler,
My soaring bring home the bacon
And also my masseur.
"Fresh,"
The mother said to her very rude son,

"Behave yourself."

"Fresh,"

The mother said to her rude son,

"Behave yourself."

"Fresh,"

The mother said to her son,

"Behave yourself."

One swan swam along

The rocky coast

And was not Zeus.

A second swan swam behind the first

Along the rocky coast

And was not Zeus.

But the third swan,

The third swan might have been

A Northern incarnation of the tyrant god.

At thunderclap of his wings

The rocks along the coast

Shiver and tremble.

Each bit of the pattern

      has its own power

To move and be moved,

      each particle

Fears the tyrant's prerogative:

To rule all as one central force.

I bend to the sensitivity in the spruce:

Self, be nothing but floods of sap

And imagination, overflow and sense.

The possible is a function of the actual
Whereas the actual has no gaps
And therefore is not possible:
At the limit of love's desolation
The Will draws smiles.
Not cruel or dismissive smiles —
Warmth looms like a mountain
That invites you to scale it —
But smiles nonetheless.
In chains of adamant language
Appearance and reality bind in embrace.
Flowers of lightening populate the sky-garden.
A crime not to chant the towers
Of learning, the delirium
That infuses us from infant to ancient.
If fable is a language of resistance
The world of animals now takes our side,
The first two swans turning to assuage us.
Tigress, making her way carefully
Towards the unknown somehow known,
The imperceptible somehow perceived,
The before and after in the present particle...

And the goddess crosses her arms over her belly.
Her eyes are mere sockets.
Her lips aren't there either
Yet seem to be pursed.
Once there was paint:
The lyre-shaped head still houses

The stone wings of a nose.

Her breasts, smooth hillocks.

Her pubic triangle, faint.

    Thank you for that silence

And that pause, O Cycladic.

The task of Earth

Is food for fish

And nothing more.

Yet the Earth

Also is fashioned divine.

Even in erasure it

Bestows a plenitude,

As Hölderlin has shown:

Cycladic goddess

Shining in her case.

Rowan trees root

By the forest-full,

Altering the calculus;

A broken tablet

Even once reassembled

Shows its fissures

And remains profane.

Also God left his instruments of creation

Outside the sauna as he entered,

And when we slip out of that box,

Perspiring heavily,

There is so much we can do with them.

The sun rises at the composition of the line.

The globe's weather warms.

Memories of the Cyclades ply our own islands.

Exiles fasten to the rocks, making new homes.

Backlots fill with new debris, with greater

      And greater forms of distress,

With more and more *kratt* material.

Mirrors fill with monsters!

Panic seeds the poem.

A shriek heard everywhere

And a dispersal to many parts.

Panic breaks the pattern,

A rift in the round,

A loss of composure.

Yet if there is anything that might be called "Nature"

Surely it is Panic, just as in the myth of Pan,

Screaming in the immensity of his solitude,

All beings hear him and are routed by fear,

Real as that separation

From the larger rhythm

We have no name for and call "Nature" as its pen.

"I's"

"Eyes"

"Skyscrapers"

Zukofsky has it,

The opacity of language

At the same time transparent.

How often does that happen in Nature?

No mention of self,

Only a lynx in the rushes.

No record of language
That is not representational.
Only the performance,
Unrecounted, referential,
Marginal, therefore creative of
Flux-ecstasy-doubt.
Finalize anything
And it becomes embalmed.
Ice in the veins
If it happens to be cold out.
Iguanas meet our gaze in the rain,
Fall from the trees when it freezes.

Geographies outside *doxa*
Flare with the marvelous.
The open sea reveals a snowy
Range jutting from its spume.
The sea swallows up
The secular totality
In instants,
Cycladic Goddess Language
Affording new encounters.
The open sea immerses all
Descriptive dross
In its murderous body.
That which cannot be depicted:
A maggot falls from my best friend's nostril.
There is actually nothing to say
And one says that nothingness

In so many ways, each one unique
And unpredictable till its last provocation.
"About which we cannot speak,
We ought to remain silent":
A dictum transgressed daily, productively,
In the silences of speech and
The speech that creates silence,
Working out our epistemology later.

3

The unknown maintains its hold
On the known. Do we know
That it is fear of homicide
That enthralls the emergent mind?
Not avalanche, not saber-toothed tiger,
Not toothless old age, not illness,
Only the prospect of being cut down
By one of one's own
Spurs consciousness's to grant
Recognition to another.
With all the fascinations of cognition
That flow from that concession.
So the fear of death is species-social, not abstract,
While death itself is deposition to a river.
But once one's ashes reach the open sea
They become susceptible to reincarnation
In a work of fiction, since all fiction
As we know, stems from the sea.

By sea, I mean language and by language
I mean your shirt, and by your shirt
I mean habitat and by habitat
I mean a shoulder holster and by shoulder holster
I mean an erratic boulder, or a field of them.
Quietly animist these small towns
Offer ample opportunity to speak with the dead
Congealed in things and ordinary words,
Thresholds of the unconscious daily crossed.
One opens a cupboard: cup and saucer.
Things resonant of who wasn't murdered,
Who dies a "natural death."
An object is a two-way mirror
We tap on the glass of to determine
If we are being watched.
Producing and dissolving distinctions
Flesh and blood forge the stream,
Contemplate the river.
The open ocean...
The indentation
From a deer hoof
In which a puddle forms...
Particulars, animal
Impressions, the face
A kind of crumbling cliff.

So time plays with space
In a sandbox filled with grapes.
Not to mention the snowstorm on the sun.

The worst blizzard anyone has seen
On the sun in many, many years:
Real accumulation though it melted fast.
Then there was the time the sun
Crashed into Granddaddy's orchard
Damaging the kumquat tree
And a blade of grass.
Back in the sky
The sun turned the color of blueberry
And gods with blue skin
The color of the sky
No longer hid themselves
In Mid-Western towns.
Even so, the sun bittern and the sun
Are two.
The sun bittern and the sun bittern
Are one and
Lay two eggs.
When the eggs are served sunny side up
The sun bittern and the sun bittern
Bitterly fly off, one day to try again,
One day perhaps to fry again the eggs.
Then there was a second snow storm
On the sun. Not so bad as the first,
Flurries really, barely anything stuck.
Then the sun turned the color of a cherry
And bathed the earth in orgasm.
The sun crashed into the pomegranate tree
In Grandma's garden,

The tree's bark was singed,
The pomegranates themselves
Were unaffected, the seeds
Remained purple jewels, gleaming once exposed.
Scientists have recently tagged
The sun, the better to track
What it does at night, when
It stays with the Russians.
Space plays with time
In a sandbox filled with lime.
In the indentation
From a deer hoof
The newly formed puddle
Turns into a pond,
Hosts the sun at new angle.
I mistake the sun for a sandpiper
And imagine it
Running ahead of the waves,
Searching for minute crustacean.
The wound is in the wood
And the bog conceals it.
The love is in the lip
And the quotidian veils it.
In the flutter of fragments
The peripheral quest,
Moses trying to put together
The original behest.
Cove populated by whispering pebbles
And rocks, sometimes in piles

Gathered for good luck by the kids.
Wives of the sea captains
Dismally fishing.

Very suddenly each word
Grows heavy to lift.
Is this due to some fatigue
Of mind, eye, hand or heart,
Or to the words themselves
Taking on more weight,
As if to signal to their bearer
One has come too close
To the growl?
Too late to signal
One's presence loudly:
One need tiptoe,
As if beside a bear.
For there is indeed a growl, a thrumming
Amidst the evenly distributed trees.
The voice of the poem animal and heavy.
One dares not to turn.
Dares not stop writing,
Each word weighted now
With tonnage and muscle.
Unbearable, really.
It lasts several measures.
Then a rain drop.
A leaf-wrinkle.
Another drop of rain.

Some other audibility of
The surrounding foliage.
A sprinkling of rain drops
And the danger has passed,
If it was danger.

Bashed shopping carts.
Discarded medical walkers
Of the infirm, the elderly.
Shards of a ripped, jagged dumpster.
An ancient carpet sweeper.
A hoe, the rusting blade of
A lawn mower.
Red wagon, also rusting.
Some wind chimes, an Ikea shelf.
A nutcracker, the leg of an iron table.
A garden whip. A deer trap.
Some rods for the drapes.
Old faucet heads, old axe heads,
A discarded tire.
Give me three of those rowan berries
And a conversation with the daemon
And of this detritus I will make
An accommodating, deadly,
Child-caring *kratt*,
An assemblage ready to do all of the work
And commit only the necessary crimes.
Give the right woman a blue skinned body
Continuous with the sky

And she will visit justice upon

The corrupt Administration,

A deity among the pols,

And among the folks committing crimes

"Just to get by."

Give us weapons and we will defend

That which need not be defended

Except for the sake of the weapons.

Give language the power

And the power of language to us

And it will use us and we will use it...

Accordingly.

After that "us" and apart from that "use"

The roseate feathers

Of the roseate spoonbill

Mirror in their shading

Traces of her lips:

Both pairs.

"I digress, and it makes me free,"

She writes in her notebook,

And also, ruefully,

"As much as I want to be,

I am never alone."

The five senses join,

Making a sixth, the five

Senses join, making a sixth,

Totaling twelve.

A broken tablet

Even once reassembled

Shows its fissures

And remains profane.

The confused angel overhead

Allows us a glimpse

And our feet touch bottom.

GLACIER TALE

The outside of the inside reveals itself to a special act of reflection.

The inside of the inside remains as impenetrable as ice.

The source and status of the so-called "special act of reflection" is not clear.

It may have to do with a recurrent sound, a recurrent chord, a certain pattern the ear begins to be able to recognize, a mimicry of the complex, all of which produce the pre-conditions for a special act of reflection.

Certainly there is a luminosity to the description of a mountain that is key to all that follows, in which the description itself becomes more than description, and the visual image and the mountain itself, the ice encasing its upper reaches, the pair of children lost near its peak and out all alone on the surface of the glacier, become almost as clear as subjectivity is obscure, almost as palpable as the children's breath turning to steam when it was earlier that afternoon invisible, almost as precious as our own lives seem to us in our most precarious moments.

There is a form of reflection which approaches itself and like perception reveals as well the faces of others, say the concerns of the two children – a boy and a girl – and the forlorn fastness of the higher altitudes.

A mountain god broods over the possibility of creating free human beings anything but beholden to himself, their troubled creator.

The children – a brother and sister – are very much on their own, singularly in the grip of their predicament, which is that of beings lost in the night.

Upon hearing the music of the god's troubled thoughts, a music that sounds freedom and determinacy, we want to say we have been listening to that music all our lives. But that isn't possible, because even thunder never claps the same way twice and the pattern shifts with every iteration.

It would be better to send an emissary to the shore of the other than to imagine one could think oneself into another world.

To send a space probe or a gondola or a poet or some other dutiful form, something or someone that could accurately deliver the message, accurately record what was said in response on that shore of the other, across all dangers bring that message back, deliver back an accurate message to the mind that had asked...

So much can go wrong. How send a space probe into the core of an apple? We are only at the beginning of fathoming anything. The musical notes that supposedly suggest the impending peal of fate suggest nothing of the kind.

Better off filling the present...the past and the future, those two drains, not so much plugged as overwhelmed by the flood of the now, a spring time cascade from off of the glacier, waters marvelously clear and refreshing, pouring in ever increasing currents, now sped up, nearly manic, demanding the present over any other tense.

The boy is older than the girl and takes the lead in trying to get them down from the heights.

Though it was he who lost the trail in the first place and led them astray, as far as the mount of the glacier...

Winter, far from spring and any cascade...

The mountain is as silent as the mind, as calm as any stone formation without hope for the future, as massive as the night.

No one doubts that this is the silence in which one steels for battle.

As the sun rises a stream of light seems to pour from the little girl's face, from the boy's face too, but less so. They do not hope, but they do not despair. They are cold, but they aren't freezing. They are lost but they haven't been lost more than a day. Having killed ennui, they are free to live or die in the heights.

The way up and the way down are the same but for them, curiously, the way up was easier.

The girl and the boy were not sent to the mountain as messengers, the whole circumstance is an accident, but they are messengers nonetheless.

A little something to eat, and some coffee...

The life of the mind and the evergreen forest have been left behind in favor of ice. Music is not about to approach the condition of language, and language is not about to approach the condition of music. At least it does not seem so, until the little girl speaks.

She has spoken before during the course of the ordeal, words of agreement with the boy, dutiful and trusting. But her new speech is different.

What she says bears upon the relationship between the visible and the invisible.

It is a simple statement and strikes the ear of the boy the way the strings of a harp might strike his ears if a harp had in fact produced the sonic vibrations.

The girl's face, lit by first sunlight, is a tone in the music. So is the girl's tightly drawn hood. The boy's face shows strain after the duress of the night.

Decision and indecision are fraught with each other's truth. Present has melted the past and precipitated the future. There is nothing left now of old habits of mind.

What does she say? The tonnage of our cynicism weighs down on the answer, straining to be released, syllable by syllable, crushing her words. Perhaps our language will not allow us to hear her, while her brother can.

What could she say? The preconditions for speech have already been set. Illusion touches the familiar and may sometimes be real.

A voice thousands of years old emanates from one's throat because of the gong in subjectivity that shatters pre-conditions, that transforms subjectivity.

A banana would be out of place on this mountain, or even talk of one, a ferris wheel has no place on this mountain, or even talk of one, "I came up here expecting a party, and no party, not even ice cream" certainly wouldn't fit, out on the ice of the glacier, in peril.

How often are we stunned into silence, how often do we crave silence, and how often do we dwell in the midst of it? Perhaps, from our perspective, she says nothing.

It isn't a laughing matter, this business of overcoming the intellect without becoming dumb.

That the children are even up on the glacier in the early morning, lost, after a long night, sheltering amidst the boulders, having lost their way in the woods on the walk back home, their parents somewhere else sick with worry, is due to the snow that fell blanketing the trail, the surprise blizzard that blinded them to the way home, the way snow abolishes the distinction between the human-altered landscape and a field of being that contains the human but is much more vast.

An undifferentiated field of marvels begging speech for differentiation into competing marvels, complimentary marvels, trail and off-trail, path and wilderness, words seeding a field of being that cups the human, the way powdered snow clings to a pine branch in a kind of equipoise if there is no wind, and tumbles sideways if there is.

No wind: repetition is ritual when it isn't anesthetic, emphasis when it isn't deadening.

No wind, and in that motionlessness the act of reflection yearns for forward motion, backward motion, lateral motion, then rests awhile from its desire to know, either tapering off in its desire to grasp being or patiently intensifying in the force of what it throws down.

Far from the mountain, school lets out in the afternoon, will open again in the morning, shouting kids celebrating release or entering trance. The little girl is on the verge of speech, addressed to her brother.

No wind: a messenger glides across a sheltered sea in a narrow boat, with a single paddle, her words a love note from one poet to another, souls in need of messenger who can move, unimpeded and uninhibited, across separating space.

Something about that boat boasts of its extra-moral status, in a quiet way one can hardly call boastful. If it is a little boastful, it is at least free of invective or moralizing posture. It is quietly sure of its linguistic mission, if we hear the word "tongue" in the word "linguistic."

A hand reaches for the form that calls out for it to reach, the "I' trembles in anticipation of discovery.

The outside of the inside reveals itself in touch and is everything, undifferentiated as an earth blanketed with cinnamon.

Reflection fails to distinguish between itself and the flesh of the other, and is glad of it.

The god broods on the fate of his grandchildren, realizing they have no fate, that he must recede.

The composer broods in the deafening storm that is modernity, music without musicians crowding out vocal chords, fingers, body and breath.

The world is will and idea, the world is still and early, the world is ill and already dead, the world is wily and filled with id, the world is all these things and none of them, increasingly luminous.

Dawn: the children near the top of the mountain. They are lost. The glacier is real. Its ice is not giving. The girl, clear-eyed, on the verge of speech...Throughout the night the boy has done much of the talking, offering instructions about the way down, reassuring his sister, remarking on how soon they will be back in their village, at home, with their parents.

Ceaselessly interrogating the real the mind is lined with feelings the way a beaver is with fur, a frigate bird with feathers.

One has been here before, the sense of the familiar as the most strange thing of all.

One has read this before, this wondering about nothing, this interrogation of the obvious, these bodies ready to ripen yet confronted by ice.

It is no dream, this dizziness of spirit, this high mountain air. Neither is it real, if the real is the sure. The kids do not even think about the risks. The boy hopes the parents will not be angry at the lateness of their eventual return. The girl's mind, filled by a question.

She, who is unquestioning of the boy, her elder brother, behind whom she has trudged through high snow most of the night, sheltered among stones up on the glacier, her eyes wide until she nearly slept – and was saved by the coffee...

The world corresponds to her eye, but not only to its capacity for sight: the eye is the tip of the sensual organism.

If the fifth element is unconcealment, earth, air, water and fire are now unconcealed as well as their representations.

If the self-arising and the arisen from elsewhere are two different forms, the need for a messenger is acute.

"During the night I could hear the ice hum," the girl says to her brother. "Did you hear it, John? Will we find our way down now? I want to hum the music for Father."

Perhaps: "John, I want to tell Mother that from the village, when we looked up at the mountain, the ice looked so far away and so old. From up close, under the stars, it seems our age, maybe even younger, so shiny. I don't think Mother knows that. But once I tell her she will be less tired at night."

Or: "John, if we perish here I hope the adults will find our bodies. I want to lie in the cemetery where Grandfather rests. But if we do get down today, or they find us soon, I want to live happily together as a family, for as long as possible. I've already been to the mountain."